A NOTE TO PARENTS

When your children are ready to "step into reading," giving them the right books is as crucial as giving them the right food to eat. **Step into Reading Books** present exciting stories and information reinforced with lively, colorful illustrations that make learning to read fun, satisfying, and worthwhile. They are priced so that acquiring an entire library of them is affordable. And they are beginning readers with a difference—they're written on five levels.

Early Step into Reading Books are designed for brand-new readers, with large type and only one or two lines of very simple text per page. **Step 1 Books** feature the same easy-to-read type as the Early Step into Reading Books, but with more words per page. **Step 2 Books** are both longer and slightly more difficult, while **Step 3 Books** introduce readers to paragraphs and fully developed plot lines. **Step 4 Books** offer exciting nonfiction for the increasingly independent reader.

The grade levels assigned to the five steps—preschool through kindergarten for the Early Books, preschool through grade 1 for Step 1, grades 1 through 3 for Step 2, grades 2 through 3 for Step 3, and grades 2 through 4 for Step 4—are intended only as guides. Some children move through all five steps very rapidly; others climb the steps over a period of several years. Either way, these books will help your child "step into reading" in style!

For my father
—M.K.

PHOTO CREDITS: page 3: Royal Geographical Society, London; page 10: Scott Polar Research Institute, Cambridge, England; page 12: Royal Geographical Society, London; page 26: Scott Polar Research Institute, Cambridge, England.

www.randomhouse.com/kids

Library of Congress Cataloging-in-Publication Data
Kulling, Monica.
Sea of ice : the wreck of the Endurance / by Monica Kulling ; illustrated by John Edens.
p. cm. — (Step into reading. Step 4 book)
SUMMARY: Describes the events of the 1914 Shackleton Antarctic expedition when, after being trapped in a frozen sea for nine months, their ship, Endurance, was finally crushed, forcing Shackleton and his men to make a very long and perilous journey across ice and stormy seas to reach inhabited land.
ISBN 0-375-80213-4 (trade) — ISBN 0-375-90213-9 (lib. bdg.)
1. Shackleton, Ernest Henry, Sir, 1874–1922—Journeys—Juvenile literature.
2. Endurance (Ship)—Juvenile literature.
3. Imperial Trans-Antarctic Expedition (1914–1917)—Juvenile literature.
[1. Imperial Trans-Antarctic Expedition (1914–1917). 2. Shackleton, Ernest Henry, Sir, 1874–1922.
3. Endurance (Ship).] I. Edens, John, ill. II. Title. III. Series.
G850 1914 .S53K85 1999 919.8904—dc21 99-19698

Printed in the United States of America 10 9 8 7 6 5 4 3 2 1

Step into Reading®

Sea of Ice

The Wreck of the ENDURANCE

By Monica Kulling
Illustrated by John Edens

A Step 4 Book

Random House  New York

Chapter One: Trapped!

January 1915: The Weddell Sea

"Keep her steady!" shouted the Boss. "The ice pack's closing in!"

The *Endurance* was in serious trouble. Ice floes rammed the ship's hull. Open water was disappearing, freezing over. Soon it would be impossible for the ship to move.

Sir Ernest Shackleton, known to his crew as "the Boss," was the leader of the Imperial Trans-Antarctic Expedition. On August 8, 1914, he and his crew had set sail from England for Antarctica. Shackleton wanted to be the first explorer to trek across the continent.

Weather in the Antarctic is severe. Wind speeds can reach 200 miles an hour. Temperatures can get as low as –100° Fahrenheit. During the Antarctic summer—from December to March—temperatures warm up. The ice pack that surrounds the continent shrinks. But this season the ice was farther north than usual.

Shackleton wanted to reach Antarctica before the end of summer, but the ice pack was locking them out. And the *Endurance* was only 85 miles from its destination—one day's sail away!

A few years earlier, Shackleton had been the first explorer to come within a hundred miles of the South Pole. He hadn't set foot on the continent, but he'd returned home a hero.

With the money he had raised for the Antarctic expedition, Shackleton bought a three-masted, coal-powered Norwegian ship. The *Endurance* was built to withstand the pressure of tons of ice. In some places, her wooden hull was more than four feet thick.

Shackleton chose his crew with care. Some were experienced sailors, while others had never been to sea before. There were a few scientists, two doctors, a carpenter, and a cook—28 men in all. There were also 69 sled dogs; two pigs; the ship's cat, Mrs. Chippy; and two years' worth of food.

The *Endurance*'s last landfall, before sailing on to Antarctica, had been South Georgia Island. The whalers on the island warned Shackleton that it was a bad year for ice. It would be best if he waited until next season. For Shackleton, going back to England was out of the question. In December 1914, he set sail for the south, in spite of the warnings.

Travel was slow. Some days the crew spotted hundreds of icebergs in 24 hours. The *Endurance* battled her way through a thousand miles of pack ice. Six weeks later, it looked as if the battle was over—and the *Endurance* was losing. Ice squeezed her on all sides. The *Endurance* lurched and stopped. She was trapped!

Chapter Two: Prisoners of Ice

The *Endurance* was stuck, as one of the men said, "like an almond in the middle of a chocolate bar." The crew tried to free the ship by chopping up the ice. But it was no use. They would have to wait for warmer temperatures to break up the ice.

To keep the men from going crazy with cabin fever, the Boss set up a schedule. Meals were at regular times. Decks were scrubbed. Seals and penguins were hunted to build up the stores for the fast-approaching winter. Even the eye sprouts on the two tons of potatoes in the hold were regularly picked out!

In the afternoon, each man was free to do what he wanted. Some read, or mended their clothes, or looked after the sled dogs. The photographer, Frank Hurley, lugged his bulky box camera up into the frozen rigging of the ship. Hurley took many photographs, which would become the visual record of the expedition.

Hubert Hudson, the navigator, took sightings of the sun and stars to keep track of the ship's location. The cook, Charles Green, was the busiest of all. He still had three meals a day to prepare!

Life on board the ice-locked *Endurance* wasn't all work. The men had singing contests to see who could sing the worst. They played cards and held dogsled races. When a bike was pulled out of the hold, there was even some acrobatic ice riding.

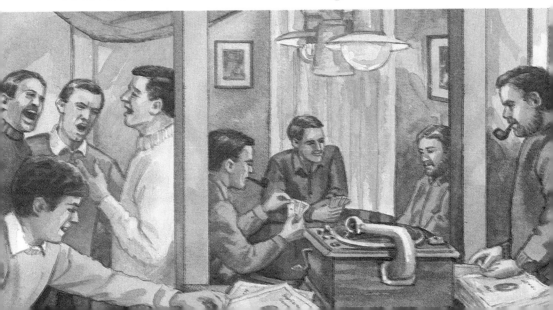

For nine months, the drift of the ice pack towed the *Endurance* farther and farther from its destination. As it moved, the pressure increased. Night and day, the crew heard the booming and grinding of the ice floes. The *Endurance* was being squeezed to its breaking point.

In private, Captain Frank Worsley told Shackleton: "If the *Endurance* has to be left behind, we will manage somehow."

But the Boss was worried. Below deck, the coal-burning stove kept them warm. The ship's thick hull kept out the wind. Could they survive on the ice if they had to abandon ship?

Finally, on October 27, 1915, the pressure from the ice pack was so great that the *Endurance* was lifted up by the blocks of shifting ice. The ship keeled over, and everything on board crashed and tumbled to one side.

Ice floes battered the ship. The decks buckled underfoot. The beams bowed overhead. Water leaked into the hold. The *Endurance* was being crushed like a nut!

Shackleton knew his ship was losing the battle. "She's going, boys," he told the crew. "It's time to get off."

Chapter Three: The *Endurance* Sinks

The men took what they could from the ship, including three small lifeboats. Shackleton's plan was to march over the frozen sea to Paulet Island, nearly 400 miles away. That's almost the distance from New York City to Niagara Falls. A hut on Paulet held stores from a previous expedition. Once they had replenished their supplies, the Boss would decide what to do next.

There was no longer enough food to feed the animals in the expedition. Mrs. Chippy, who was really a tomcat, had to be shot or he would have been quickly killed by the dogs. Many of the dogs were also shot—even the puppies.

The crew had to leave most of their belongings behind. Each man was allowed only two pounds of personal gear. The lifeboats were heavy enough with the bare essentials. Each boat weighed almost 1,000 pounds when loaded.

The frozen sea was heaped with ice blocks, and it was snowing heavily. Dragging the lifeboats was hard work. It took 15 men to drag one boat a few inches at a time. In some places, the landscape looked as if the waves had frozen in place. The men sank up to their hips in wet snow. Their boots filled with icy water. They were freezing and exhausted.

It was no wonder that Shackleton ordered the men to stop after they had been hauling the boats for two hours. They had made very little progress. The wreck of the *Endurance* was only one and a half miles away. They would camp on the ice and wait for it to break up. Then they could launch the lifeboats. They set up tents and continued the day-to-day life of surviving a South Pole winter.

On November 21, 1915, Shackleton and his men bade farewell to the ship that had taken them to the bottom of the world. They stood on an ice hill and watched as the three masts slowly sank. Suddenly the ship plunged. A rush of ice buried her, and then silence filled the air.

The *Endurance* had been the last link to the outside world. Now the men were completely alone. But what was even worse, no one knew they were stranded.

Chapter Four: Land at Last!

April 1916

"Crack! Crack!" shouted Shackleton, giving the signal. Everyone knew what that meant. The ice floe they were on was splitting in half—right through the camp! The breakup of the ice had started.

The men raced to save boats and supplies. Several jumped over a gap in the ice to save their supply of meat. If the food drifted off, there would be nothing to live on, since the penguins they once hunted had migrated for the season. After minutes of anxious work, everything was safe on the same ice floe.

A few days later, the ice floe broke again. Now there were patches of open water. Shackleton gave the order to launch. The lifeboats were dragged to the edge and pushed into the water. The men quickly rowed away from the ice floe that had been their prison for months.

In the largest boat, the *James Caird*, Shackleton set a course for a sliver of land 200 miles away called Elephant Island. Day and night he stood at the tiller. He knew that his men needed to see him in charge. He also knew that if they missed Elephant Island, the next landfall was thousands of miles away. They would *never* survive!

Waves crashed into the open boats. Four men rowed while the others bailed out the water. Their ragged clothes weren't waterproof and quickly froze into an icy armor. Hands and feet stung with the cold.

The men had no drinking water. The constant spray of salty water made their mouths swell up until their lips bled. Frozen, raw seal meat gave them some relief from dehydration.

Killer whales were a constant threat. They trailed the boats, waiting for any man unlucky enough to fall overboard.

For seven sleepless days and nights, the

men braved the bitter cold and raging storms of the South Atlantic Ocean.

One morning, the ice peaks of Elephant Island finally came into view. The island was only 30 miles away.

"Congratulations, Worsley!" Shackleton shouted. "You've steered us true."

The shoreline was unwelcoming. Dark cliffs rose high above a rocky coast. Wind

and waves made the landing treacherous. After several attempts, the boats finally found solid ground.

The men staggered onto the shore. They hadn't stood on land for over a year! Some men fell to their knees and kissed the ground. Others ran down the beach, laughing and crying. They had survived. No one could know the dangers that still lay ahead.

Chapter Five: Back at Sea

The cook immediately set up his blubber-heated stove to boil milk. The men drank it piping hot to get their blood flowing again.

Elephant Island was barren and stormy. The mountain peaks were covered with glaciers. In the days to come, howling winds would shred tents and blow away blankets and cooking utensils. It was not a place to stay for long.

Shackleton knew that Elephant Island was deserted. No one was going to rescue them. They would have to launch the largest boat and head back for South Georgia Island, where the whaling station was.

But the crew was totally exhausted. Many of the men needed medical attention. Two had frostbitten feet and could barely walk. One had collapsed onshore with a heart attack.

"We can't stay here," whispered Shackleton. His voice was hoarse from all the shouting he'd done on the open sea. "But we can't all go on. Some will have to stay behind."

Shackleton chose five men and prepared to set sail. The whaling station in Stromness Bay was their only hope. But first they faced an 800-mile trip through the South Atlantic Ocean—the stormiest ocean on earth.

South Atlantic waves are called Cape Horn rollers. There is no land to break their flow, so they build to great heights and speeds. An open lifeboat is no match for these waves. But Shackleton knew there was no other choice.

On the morning of April 24, the *James Caird* was loaded with six weeks' worth of food, six sleeping bags, and 1,000 pounds of beach stones to add weight to the boat for stability. Shackleton shook each man's hand.

"Good luck, Boss," called the men as the boat left the shore.

The 22 men left behind made a hut out of the two remaining boats and took shelter. They ate penguins and seals to survive. They would live with terrible loneliness and the constant threat of death. But every man believed Shackleton would do all he could to save them. Each day they looked for his return.

Meanwhile, Shackleton and his small crew were fighting for their lives in the ocean. Their greatest danger was an old enemy—ice. Icebergs and ice floes were especially hazardous at night.

For the first two days, the wind drove the *Caird* toward South Georgia Island. But on the third day, their luck ran out. Torrents of rain fell. The wind was pushing them *away* from South Georgia.

"This is it, boys," said Shackleton above the howling wind. "We'll have to fight it out."

The boat pitched and rolled. The helmsman steered in a zigzag to stay on course. Waves drenched the men and filled the boat. Soon the sails and oars were caked with ice. The men had to shift the stones at the bottom of the boat to keep it from tipping over.

Hour after hour, they fought the ocean. Would this be the end of their rescue mission? Was this the final disaster?

"We should see the island by now," muttered Worsley.

The men's throats were raw with thirst. The second keg of water was undrinkable. If they didn't reach South Georgia soon, they would all die.

Suddenly one of the men saw something floating past the boat.

"Look," he said hoarsely. "Seaweed."

That meant land was close!

A cormorant flew overhead. This seabird never flies more than 15 miles from land. Soon the snowy peaks of South Georgia came into view. *They had made it!*

Later Shackleton remembered the amazing boat journey. "We were a tiny speck in a great big sea," he wrote. "One moment we thought we were going to die. The next moment hope would rise on the crest of a wave."

Chapter Six: An Overland Hike

The boat landed on the rocky shore of South Georgia Island. Two of the men were sick. They were too weak to move. It was decided that one sailor would stay behind to look after them, and Frank Worsley and Thomas Crean would hike with Shackleton across the island to the whaling station.

On a night when the moon was bright, the three men started climbing a steep, snow-covered slope. No one had ever explored the interior of the island before. There was no way of knowing what the land was like. Their map only showed the coastline.

The men scaled treacherous peaks with

only 50 feet of rope and a carpenter's tool used to chop footholds in the ice. Sometimes they climbed peaks that led nowhere. When this happened, they had to retrace their steps and start over. They climbed all night and all the next day.

At the top of one peak, Shackleton stopped. The valley below was thick with fog. Daylight was fading. The wind was getting stronger. It would take hours to climb down this slope. If they were caught on the mountaintop at night, they could freeze to death. The winds are coldest and strongest on the summit of a mountain.

Shackleton had an idea.

"We'll slide down," he said.

Worsley and Crean looked at each other. Was the Boss joking? Was he actually suggesting something so dangerous? They might hit a boulder or go crashing into a ravine. There was no way to tell what lay at the bottom of this slope.

But Shackleton wasn't joking. He instructed the men to coil the rope into three mats for seating. Then he tied the rest of the rope between them. The men looked like they were ready for a toboggan run—without a toboggan!

Shackleton didn't wait for second thoughts. He kicked off. The three shot down the slope over ice and snow, picking up speed. At the bottom, the slope leveled off and the men came to a dead stop in a snowbank. It was a soft landing for a dangerous ride. The men brushed the snow off, laughing with relief.

From the top of the last ridge, Stromness Bay could be seen in the distance.

"It looks too good to be true," said Worsley, out of breath.

The blast of the whaling station's whistle carried on the icy air. The men were reminded of the days they had spent on the island almost two years earlier. The hike overland was nearly over. With newfound energy, the climbers started down the steep, icy face of their last glacier.

Chapter Seven: The Rescue

Three weary men with long hair and beards walked into the whaling station. Their ragged and worn-out appearance made everyone stop working. No one had ever come from the interior of the island. Visitors always arrived by boat.

Shackleton knocked on the foreman's door. When it opened, he said softly, "My name is Shackleton."

The foreman was stunned. Like most of the world, he believed that the *Endurance* had been lost at sea. A rescue ship, the *Aurora,* had also gotten trapped in the ice but had made it to New Zealand. When a message from the *Aurora* reached England,

the newspapers printed the headline: IS
SHACKLETON SAFE?

It was assumed that no one could survive
months in the harshest climate on earth.

The foreman recovered from his shock and ordered his workers to make the survivors comfortable. The men enjoyed long, hot baths. They shaved and put on new clothes. After a hearty meal, Worsley boarded a whaling ship for the other side of the island to pick up the others.

Meanwhile, the Boss arranged for a ship to rescue the 22 men left on Elephant Island. The ship would leave the next day. That night, the whalers had a party for the brave men who had sailed a boat through the most dangerous waters on earth. Everyone wanted to shake their hands.

The next day, Shackleton left for Elephant Island aboard the rescue ship. Within a week, he was stopped by ice and had to return to port. A second ship was also stopped by ice, and so was a third.

Shackleton was getting more and more anxious. He contacted the British government and asked for a ship strong enough to plow through the ice. They told him a ship called the *Discovery* was on its way, but it would take weeks to reach him. Shackleton knew that the men on Elephant Island didn't have much more time.

South America was closer, so Shackleton asked the Chilean government for a ship. The steel-hulled ship, the *Yelcho,* wasn't built to take ice, but Shackleton didn't let that stop him. He set sail on August 25.

For five days, the *Yelcho* steered through ice floes and icebergs. Then, on August 30, the peaks of Elephant Island came into view. Shackleton had made it!

Chapter Eight: Shackleton Returns

The men on the island had finally given up hope that Shackleton would ever return. Still, each morning a man would climb a nearby bluff to check the ocean. It was a habit that no one wanted to break.

That morning, Marston was on top of the bluff when he spotted what looked like a ship in the distance. He ran back to camp to tell the others.

"I think we better send up some smoke signals," he said, clearly excited.

At first there was silence. No one seemed to know what Marston was talking about. Then everyone realized at once that a ship had been sighted. They all scrambled out of the makeshift hut and headed for the bluff. Some stopped to put on boots, but most went as they were.

Sure enough, there was a ship. It was just a dot on the horizon, but it was getting closer by the minute.

Hurley gathered dry grass. He poured blubber oil on the grass and lit it. Black smoke filled the air.

Soon the *Yelcho* was near enough for Shackleton to be heard.

"Is everyone all right?" he shouted.

"Everyone is well" came the reply.

It was a miracle. Every single man had survived.

Shackleton and his men returned home to a country at war. Millions of young men were fighting and dying in World War I. England hardly seemed interested in Shackleton's story. He and his crew had survived the most daring Antarctic adventure in history. They had mastered one hardship after another. It was Shackleton's bravery and leadership that had brought everyone safely home.

The ordeal was over. Shackleton should have been relieved and happy to be home. But the allure of the South Pole drew him like a magnet.

In 1921, Shackleton put together another expedition. It wasn't clear what the goal was. One plan was to sail around Antarctica and map all the islands. An even more exciting

plan was to search for Captain Kidd's pirate treasure. Whichever goal it was, the voyage would be Shackleton's last.

On January 4, 1922, Shackleton landed on South Georgia Island. He was warmly greeted by the whalers. Sadly, that night in his cabin, Shackleton died of a heart attack. He was buried on the island, in the part of the world that he loved best. The wild beauty of the Antarctic surrounds him in his final resting place.